～ Book 1 ～

PIANO MUSIC BY WOMEN COMPOSERS

40 Upper Elementary to Early Intermediate Level Pieces

Compiled and Edited by Immanuela Gruenberg

ISBN 978-1-70514-752-8

Visit Hal Leonard Online at
www.halleonard.com

World headquarters, contact:
Hal Leonard
7777 West Bluemound Road
Milwaukee, WI 53213
Email: info@halleonard.com

In Europe, contact:
Hal Leonard Europe Limited
1 Red Place
London, W1K 6PL
Email: info@halleonardeurope.com

In Australia, contact:
Hal Leonard Australia Pty. Ltd.
4 Lentara Court
Cheltenham, Victoria, 3192 Australia
Email: info@halleonard.com.au

PREFACE

Upon embarking on this project, I had little idea of what I would find. There were, of course, the "usual suspects:" women composers whose names and whose music have stood the test of time and are familiar to many. There were also those whose names ring a bell but whose music does not. The real unknowns were, well, the unknowns. How many women composers whose music is worth studying and listening to were out there? Adding to the puzzle was the fact this project took place during the COVID-19 pandemic when libraries were closed, reducing the number and type of sources I had access to. By the time I had to make the final decision on what to include in these two volumes, I had five times as much music as could be included within the allotted space. This meant that I had to leave out eighty percent of the music I had collected.

When selecting the twenty percent to be included, I searched for the following: beautiful, interesting compositions that students can benefit from and will love learning, teachers will enjoy teaching, and audiences will appreciate; a variety to styles, composers, and nationalities; showcasing as many composers as possible, while striking a balance between well-known, lesser known, and unknown composers. With these considerations in mind, I chose mostly shorter works.

—*Immanuela Gruenberg*

CONTENTS

AMY BEACH

6   Promenade in C Major, *Children's Carnival*, Op. 25, No. 1

9   Pantalon, *Children's Carnival*, Op. 25, No. 3

12   Pierrot and Pierrette, *Children's Carnival*, Op. 25, No. 4

14   Secrets, *Children's Carnival*, Op. 25, No. 5

17   Harlequin, *Children's Carnival*, Op. 25, No. 6

20   Minuet in F Major, *Children's Album*, Op. 36, No. 1

22   Gavotte in D minor, *Children's Album*, Op. 36, No. 2

24   Waltz in C Major, *Children's Album*, Op. 36, No. 3

MÉLANIE BONIS

26   Aubade in D Major, *Children's Scenes*, Op. 92, No. 1

30   Hide and Seek, *Children's Scenes*, Op. 92, No. 3

33   Slow Waltz in C Major, *Children's Scenes*, Op. 92, No. 4

36   Frère Jacques, *Children's Scenes*, Op. 92, No. 6

CÉCILE CHAMINADE

38   Prelude in C Major,
Children's Album (Volume 1), Op. 123, No. 1

40   Intermezzo in G Major,
Children's Album (Volume 1), Op. 123, No. 2

42   Canzonetta in C Major,
Children's Album (Volume 1), Op. 123, No. 3

44   Rondeau in F Major,
Children's Album (Volume 1), Op. 123, No. 4

46   Gavotte in A minor,
Children's Album (Volume 1), Op. 123, No. 5

48   Gigue in C Major,
Children's Album (Volume 1), Op. 123, No. 6

50   Romance in F Major,
Children's Album (Volume 1), Op. 123, No. 7

52   Barcarolle in A Major,
Children's Album (Volume 1), Op. 123, No. 8

54   Orientale in E minor,
Children's Album (Volume 1), Op. 123, No. 9

57   Air de Ballet,
Children's Album (Volume 1), Op. 123, No. 11

60   Marche Russe in D minor,
Children's Album (Volume 1), Op. 123, No. 12

62   Idylle in C Major,
Children's Album (Volume 2), Op. 126, No. 1

64   Aubade in E Major,
Children's Album (Volume 2), Op. 126, No. 2

FREDRIKKE EGEBERG

66   Adagio cantabile,
Six Songs Without Words for Piano

68   Religioso,
Six Songs Without Words for Piano

LOUISE FARRENC

70   Etude in C Major,
25 Easy Etudes, Op. 50, No. 1

72   Etude in A minor,
25 Easy Etudes, Op. 50, No. 2

74   Etude in G Major,
25 Easy Etudes, Op. 50, No. 3

76   Etude in C Major,
25 Easy Etudes, Op. 50, No. 12

78   Etude in C Major,
25 Easy Etudes, Op. 50, No. 14

80   Etude in C Major,
25 Easy Etudes, Op. 50, No. 16

82   Etude in F-sharp Major,
25 Intermediate Etudes, Op. 42, No. 19

EMMA HARTMANN

85   Piano Piece in C Major,
Piano Pieces, Op. Posthumous, No. 2

86   Viennese Waltz in G Major,
Piano Pieces, Op. Posthumous, No. 5

MARIE JAËLL

88   After the Waltz, *The Good Days*

CLARA SCHUMANN

90   Prelude No. 1 in C Major,
Simple Preludes for Students

90   Prelude No. 2 in A-flat Major,
Simple Preludes for Students

ANNA STUBENBERG

91   Austrian Dance in A-flat Major,
The People of Kapfenberg, Op. 67, No. 2

COMPOSER BIOGRAPHIES

Born in New Hampshire, American composer and pianist **Amy Beach** (1867–1944) achieved great success as both pianist and composer. She started piano lessons at age six and began composing at a very young age. She appeared as soloist with orchestra and in solo recitals, performing her own compositions alongside the classical repertoire. Upon her marriage to Dr. H. H. A. Beach, a physician and amateur singer, she cut back on her concert tours and devoted her time to composing. Her composition studies consisted of no more than one year of harmony and counterpoint. Upon the advice of Wilhelm Gericke, she spent ten years studying the masters, teaching herself fugue, orchestration, theory, and so on. In 1911 she traveled to Europe to promote the sale of her compositions and again make a name for herself as a performer. Both her compositions and her pianism were very well received. She returned to the US at the breakout of World War I. Amy Beach composed solo, chamber, orchestral, and choral works that were performed with great success and to critical acclaim unprecedented for a woman composer in the US at the time.

French composer **Mélanie Bonis** (1858–1937) studied organ with César Franck, and harmony with Ernest Guiraud at the Paris Conservatoire. She married in 1883 and for about ten years devoted herself to raising a family. Bonis composed over 300 works, about half of them piano compositions, the others organ, chamber, choral, and orchestra works. Most of her music was published during her lifetime. In 1907 she became a member of the committee of the *Société des compositeurs de musique* and from 1910 to 1914 served as its secretary.

Born in Paris, **Cécile Chaminade** (1857–1944) was a successful pianist and composer. She studied privately with Félix Le Couppey, Marmontel, and Benjamin Godard. She composed mainly character pieces. These were very successful both with audiences and financially. She toured France, was a favorite of queen Victoria, and in 1908 she toured the United States, performing in 12 cities. In 1913 she became the first female composer to be granted admission to the Order of the Legion of Honor. Of her approximately 400 compositions, almost all of which were published during her lifetime, the majority are piano works. The rest are songs, an opera, a ballet, and orchestral suites. Her compositions were enormously successful with both critics and audiences.

Fredrikke Egeberg (1815–1861) was a Norwegian pianist and composer. She was the youngest of nine children and the only daughter. Several of her family members, including some of her siblings, became professional and amateur musicians. She composed piano music, songs, and choral works.

Louise Farrenc (1804–1875) was a French composer, pianist, scholar, and teacher. She studied piano with a student of Clementi and later with Ignaz Moscheles and Johann Nepomuk Hummel. At age fifteen she entered the Paris Conservatoire to study composition with Anton Reicha. In 1821 she married flutist

Aristide Farrenc with whom she collaborated in concerts and in her research. He also published her early compositions. These received high praise from Schumann in his *Neue Zeitschrift für Musik*. In 1842 she was appointed Professor of Piano at the Paris Conservatoire, a position she held until 1873. Many of her students won competitions and became professional musicians. In an effort to revive 17th and 18th century music, she and her students organized and performed concert featuring that music. Her research on that topic was published in *Le trésor des pianists*. She composed mainly for the piano, but also chamber works, choral music, and symphonies. In 1845, her piano etudes became required repertoire at the Conservatoire.

Danish composer **Emma Hartmann** (1807–1851) composed under the pseudonym Frederik H. Palmer. She was married to Emilius Hartmann who came from a German-origin Danish family of musicians. Emma Hartmann's first published composition was originally composed for a Student Association dance. Later publications included 22 *Romances and Songs*. In 1908, a collection of her piano pieces was published by her son, Frederik Hartmann.

Marie Jaëll (1846–1925), also known by her maiden name, Marie Trautmann, was a French pianist, composer, and pedagogue. She studied with Ignaz Moscheles, Heinrich Herz, and Franz Liszt, and started preforming at a very young age. At twenty she married pianist Alfred Jaëll, with whom she performed and who apparently also helped with her career. She was a successful pianist, and the first French pianist to perform the complete Beethoven piano sonatas. Saint-Saëns dedicated to her his first piano concerto and the *Etude en forme de valse*. Her compositions were published and were well received. As a pedagogue, Marie Jaëll developed a method of playing based on her scientific analysis of how the muscles work. Her aim was to make technique and artistry work synergistically, combining technical elements with artistic ones. In addition, she encouraged performers to develop the ability to create a mental image of the sought-after sound. Her method became known as The Jaëll Method.

Clara Schumann (1819–1896) was a German pianist, composer, and teacher. She was one of the leading piano virtuosos of the 19th century and the teacher of many professional pianists. She started piano lessons with her mother Mariane, herself a gifted singer and pianist who had appeared as solo singer, and was the piano soloist in John Field's second piano concerto at the Leipzig Gewandhaus. When, following her parents' divorce, her father Friedrich Wieck gained full custody, she studied with him, receiving a thorough musical education in a highly disciplined environment. Wieck Schumann toured from a young age and continued concertizing into her sixties, playing solo recitals, chamber concerts, and as soloist with orchestras. At 21, and against her father's wishes, she married Robert Schumann, whose works she later edited for Breitkopf & Härtel. Her compositions include a large number of solo piano works as well as lieder, concertos, chamber music, and arrangements.

Anna Stubenberg (1821–1912) was born in Austria to an old noble family. Her father was Count Gustav Adolph von Stubenberg. She grew up in Pest, Hungary, where she studied music, art, and languages. She was known as a gifted improviser. She composed short piano pieces such as dances and marches and Lieder.

Promenade in C Major
Children's Carnival, Op. 25, No. 1

Amy Beach
(1867–1944)

Editorial fingering suggestions in parentheses.

Pantalon
Children's Carnival, Op. 25, No. 3

Amy Beach
(1867–1944)

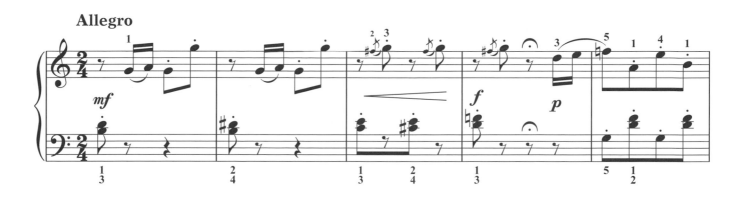

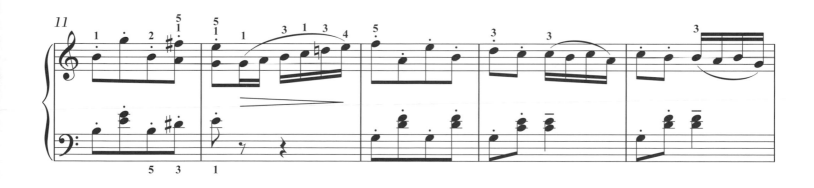

Pierrot and Pierrette

Children's Carnival, Op. 25, No. 4

Amy Beach
(1867–1944)

Tempo di Valse

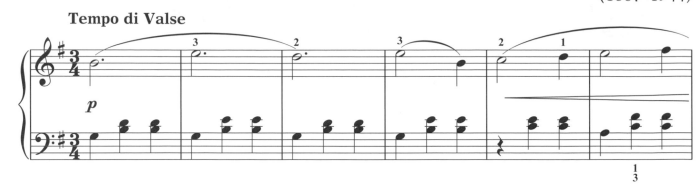

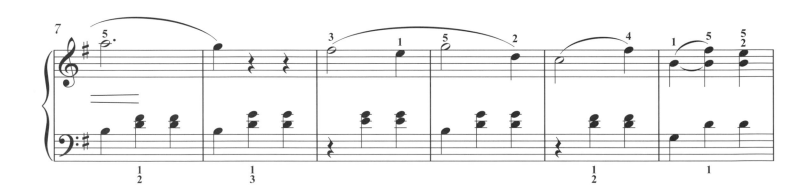

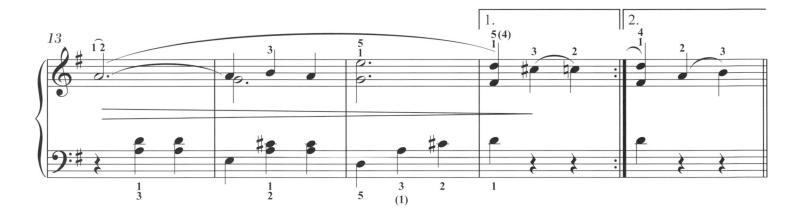

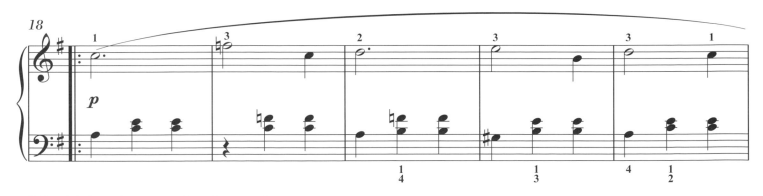

Editorial fingering suggestions in parentheses.

Secrets

Children's Carnival, Op. 25, No. 5

Amy Beach
(1867–1944)

This page is intentionally left blank to facilitate page turns.

Harlequin
Children's Carnival, Op. 25, No. 6

Amy Beach
(1867–1944)

Minuet in F Major

Children's Album, Op. 36, No. 1

Amy Beach
(1867–1944)

Gavotte in D minor
Children's Album, Op. 36, No. 2

Amy Beach
(1867–1944)

Waltz in C Major

Children's Album, Op. 36, No. 3

Amy Beach
(1867–1944)

Editorial fingering suggestions in parentheses.

to Odette Dubosc

Aubade in D Major

from *Children's Scenes*, Op. 92, No. 1

Mélanie Bonis
(1858–1937)

Allegretto con moto

"Wake up, Odette!"

"Come, play in the garden!"

bring out bass

Editorial fingering suggestions in parentheses.

"Do you not hear the

birds singing?"

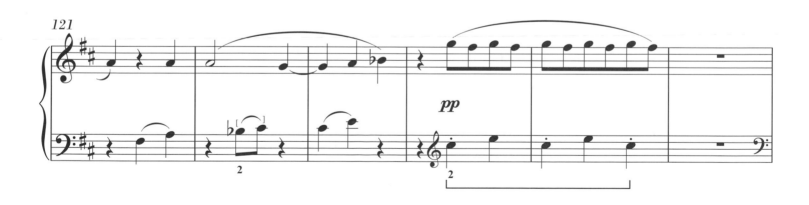

to Francoise Duroyaume

Hide and Seek
Children's Scenes, Op. 92, No. 3

Mélanie Bonis
(1858–1937)

Editorial fingering suggestions in parentheses.

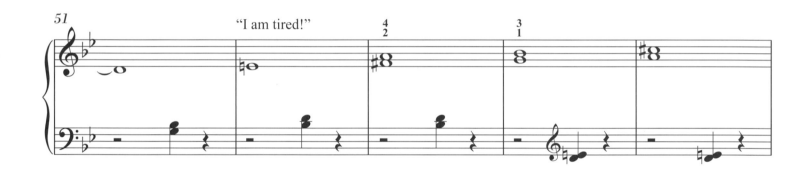

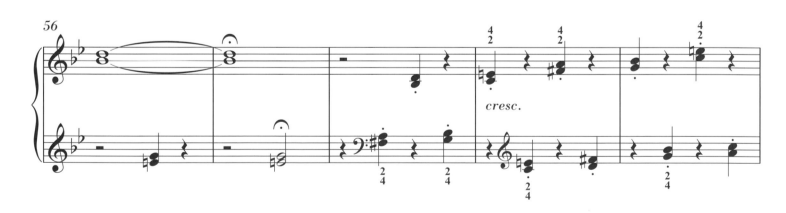

to Max Domange

Slow Waltz in C Major

Children's Scenes, Op. 92, No. 4

Mélanie Bonis
(1858–1937)

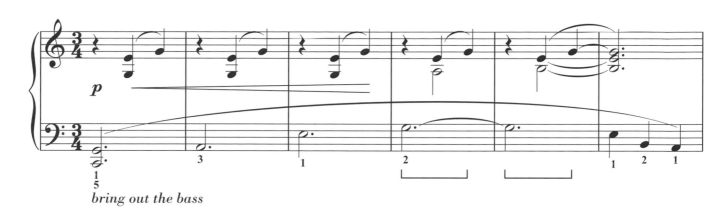

bring out the bass

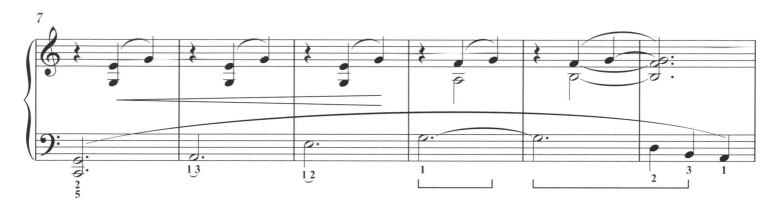

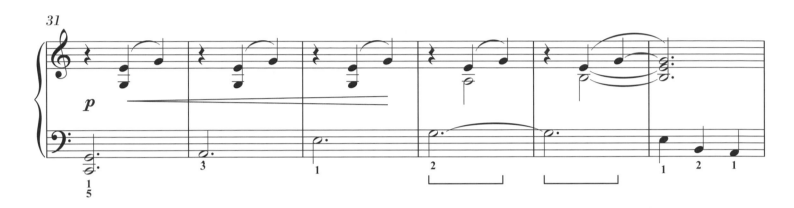

to Jean Duroyaume

Frère Jacques

Children's Scenes, Op. 92, No. 6

Mélanie Bonis
(1858–1937)

Editorial fingering suggestions are in parentheses.

Prelude in C Major

Children's Album (Volume 1), Op. 123, No. 1

Cécile Chaminade
(1857–1944)

Fingerings are editorial suggestions.

Intermezzo in G Major
Children's Album (Volume 1), Op. 123, No. 2

Cécile Chaminade
(1857–1944)

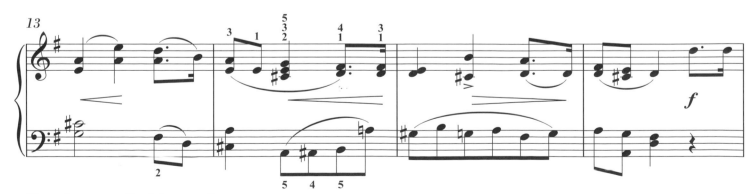

Fingerings are editorial suggestions.

Canzonetta in C Major
Children's Album (Volume 1), Op. 123, No. 3

Cécile Chaminade
(1857–1944)

Fingerings are editorial suggestions.

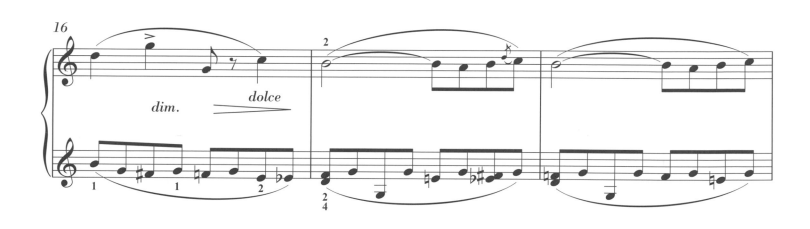

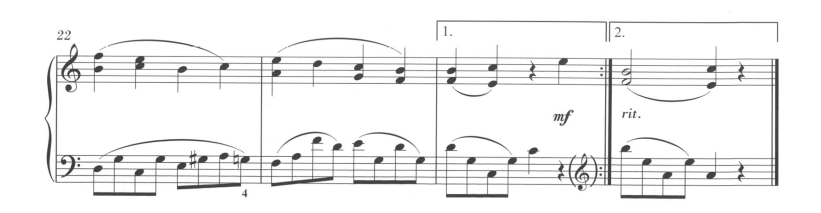

Rondeau in F Major
Children's Album (Volume 1), Op. 123, No. 4

Cécile Chaminade
(1857–1944)

Fingerings are editorial suggestions.

Gavotte in A minor
Children's Album (Volume 1), Op. 123, No. 5

Cécile Chaminade
(1857–1944)

Fingerings are editorial suggestions.

Gigue in C Major
Children's Album (Volume 1), Op. 123, No. 6

Cécile Chaminade
(1857–1944)

Fingerings are editorial suggestions.

Romance in F Major
Children's Album (Volume 1), Op. 123, No. 7

Cécile Chaminade
(1857–1944)

Fingerings are editorial suggestions.

Barcarolle in A Major
Children's Album (Volume 1), Op. 123, No. 8

Cécile Chaminade
(1857–1944)

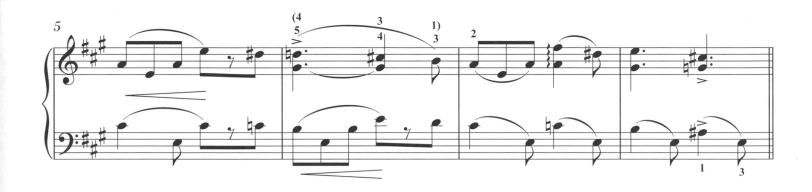

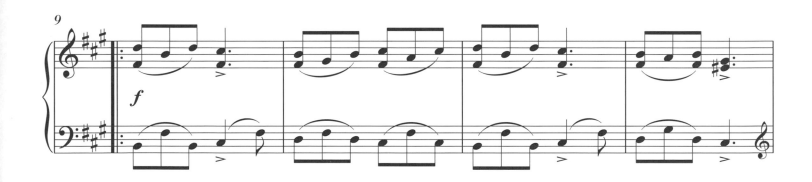

Fingerings are editorial suggestions.

* These fingerings appear in the source.

Orientale in E minor
Children's Album (Volume 1), Op. 123, No. 9

Cécile Chaminade
(1857–1944)

Fingerings are editorial suggestions.

This page is intentionally left blank to facilitate page turns.

Air de Ballet

Children's Album (Volume 1), Op. 123, No. 11

Cécile Chaminade
(1857–1944)

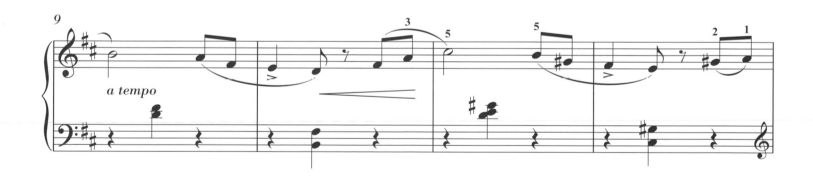

Fingerings are editorial suggestions.

Marche Russe in D minor

Children's Album (Volume 1), Op. 123, No. 12

Cécile Chaminade
(1857–1944)

Fingerings are editorial suggestions.

to Marie-Louise Promio

Idylle in C Major
Children's Album (Volume 2), Op. 126, No. 1

Cécile Chaminade
(1857–1944)

Fingerings are editorial suggestions, except those marked with an asterisk.

to Jean Béchet

Aubade in E Major

Children's Album (Volume 2), Op. 126, No. 2

Cécile Chaminade
(1857–1944)

The melody sustained but brought out.

Fingerings are editorial suggestions.

Adagio cantabile
Six Songs Without Words for Piano

Fredrikke Egeberg
(1815–1861)

Fingerings are editorial suggestions.

Religioso
Six Songs Without Words for Piano

Fredrikke Egeberg
(1815–1861)

Fingerings are editorial suggestions.

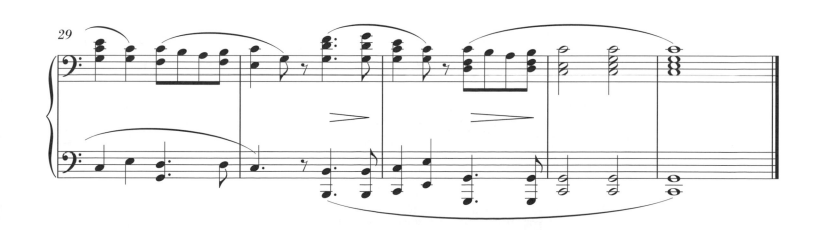

Etude in C Major

25 Easy Etudes, Op. 50, No. 1

Louise Farrenc
(1804–1875)

Andante grazioso

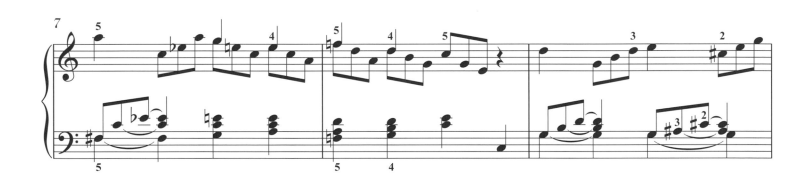

Etude in A minor
25 Easy Etudes, Op. 50, No. 2

Louise Farrenc
(1804–1875)

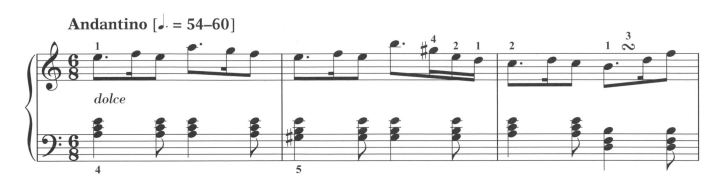

Etude in G Major

25 Easy Etudes, Op. 50, No. 3

Louise Farrenc
(1804–1875)

Etude in C Major

25 Easy Etudes, Op. 50, No. 12

Louise Farrenc
(1804–1875)

Etude in C Major
25 Easy Etudes, Op. 50, No. 14

Louise Farrenc
(1804–1875)

Etude in C Major
25 Easy Etudes, Op. 50, No. 16

Louise Farrenc
(1804–1875)

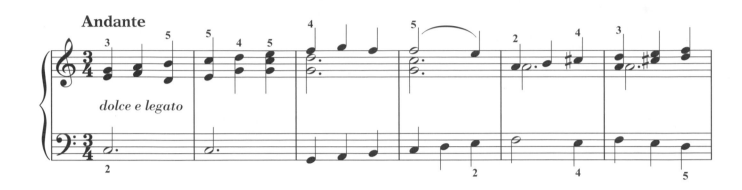

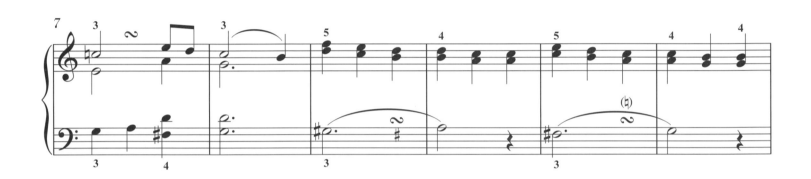

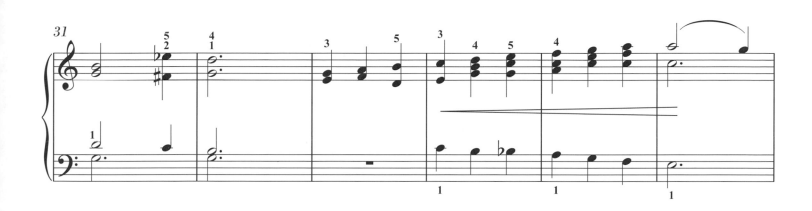

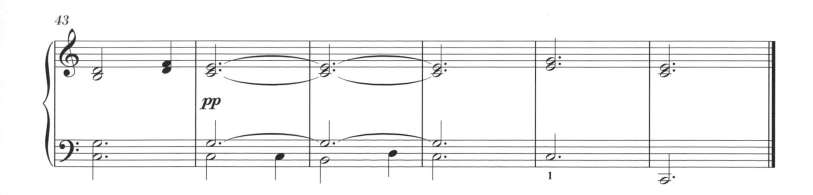

Etude in F-sharp Major
25 Intermediate Etudes, Op. 42, No. 19

Louise Farrenc
(1804–1875)

Adagio religioso, molto legato

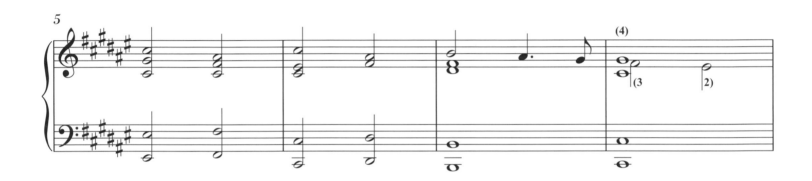

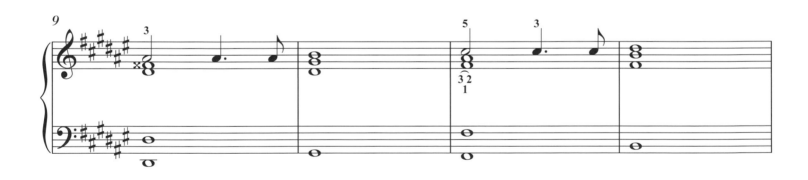

Editorial fingering suggestions in parentheses.

This page is intentionally left blank to facilitate page turns.

Piano Piece in C Major
Piano Pieces, Op. Posthumous, No. 2

Emma Hartman
(1807–1851)

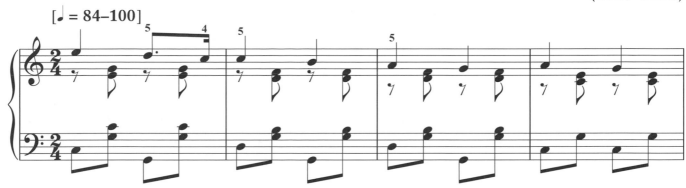

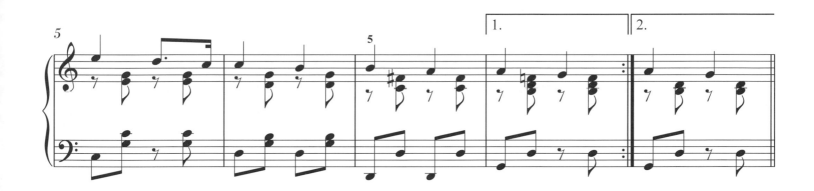

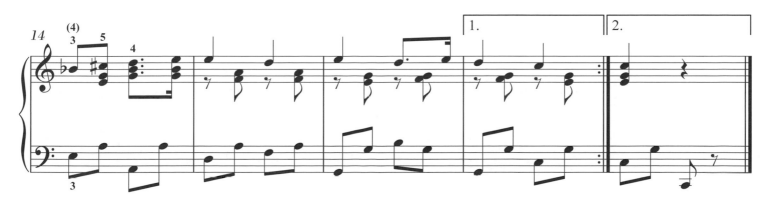

Fingerings are editorial suggestions.

Viennese Waltz in G Major
Piano Pieces, Op. Posthumous, No. 5

Emma Hartman
(1807–1851)

Fingerings are editorial suggestions.

After the Waltz

The Good Days

Marie Jaëll
(1846–1925)

Mouvement de valse

Fingerings are editorial suggestions.

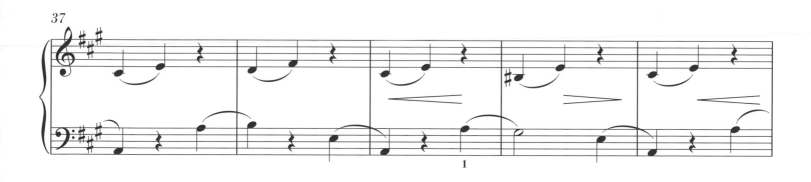

Prelude No. 1 in C Major

Simple Preludes for Students

Clara Schumann
(1819–1896)

Fingerings are editorial suggestions.

Prelude No. 2 in A-flat Major

Simple Preludes for Students

Clara Schumann
(1819–1896)

Fingerings are editorial suggestions.

dedicated to Wolfgang Herr and Graf zu Stubenberg

Austrian Dance in A-flat Major

The People of Kapfenberg, Op. 67, No. 2

Anna Stubenberg
(1821–1912)

Fingerings are editorial suggestions.